THE CHILDREN'S HOUR

FRANCIS THOMPSON

FATHER TABB

FATHER VINCENT McNABB, O.P.

KATHARINE TYNAN HINKSON

THE CHILDREN'S HOUR
OF HEAVEN ON EARTH

With Pictures by
LINDSAY D. SYMINGTON
and a Talk, with Tales and Texts,
by Fr. VINCENT McNABB, O.P.

Catholic Authors Press
www.CatholicAuthors.com

BETWEEN the dark and the daylight,
   When the night is beginning to lower,
   Comes a pause in the day's occupation,
   That is known as the Children's Hour.
                              Longfellow.

CONTENTS

Dedication

Little Jesus *By Francis Thompson* 7

The Little Scholar *By S. Baring-Gould* 11

At Prayer *By Katharine Tynan Hinkson* 16

Creation's Catechism *By Wilfrid Meynell* 17

St. Teresa and the Child *By Father Tabb* 20

Out of Bounds - *By Father Tabb* 21

And a Talk, with Tales and Texts,
By Father Vincent McNabb, O.P.

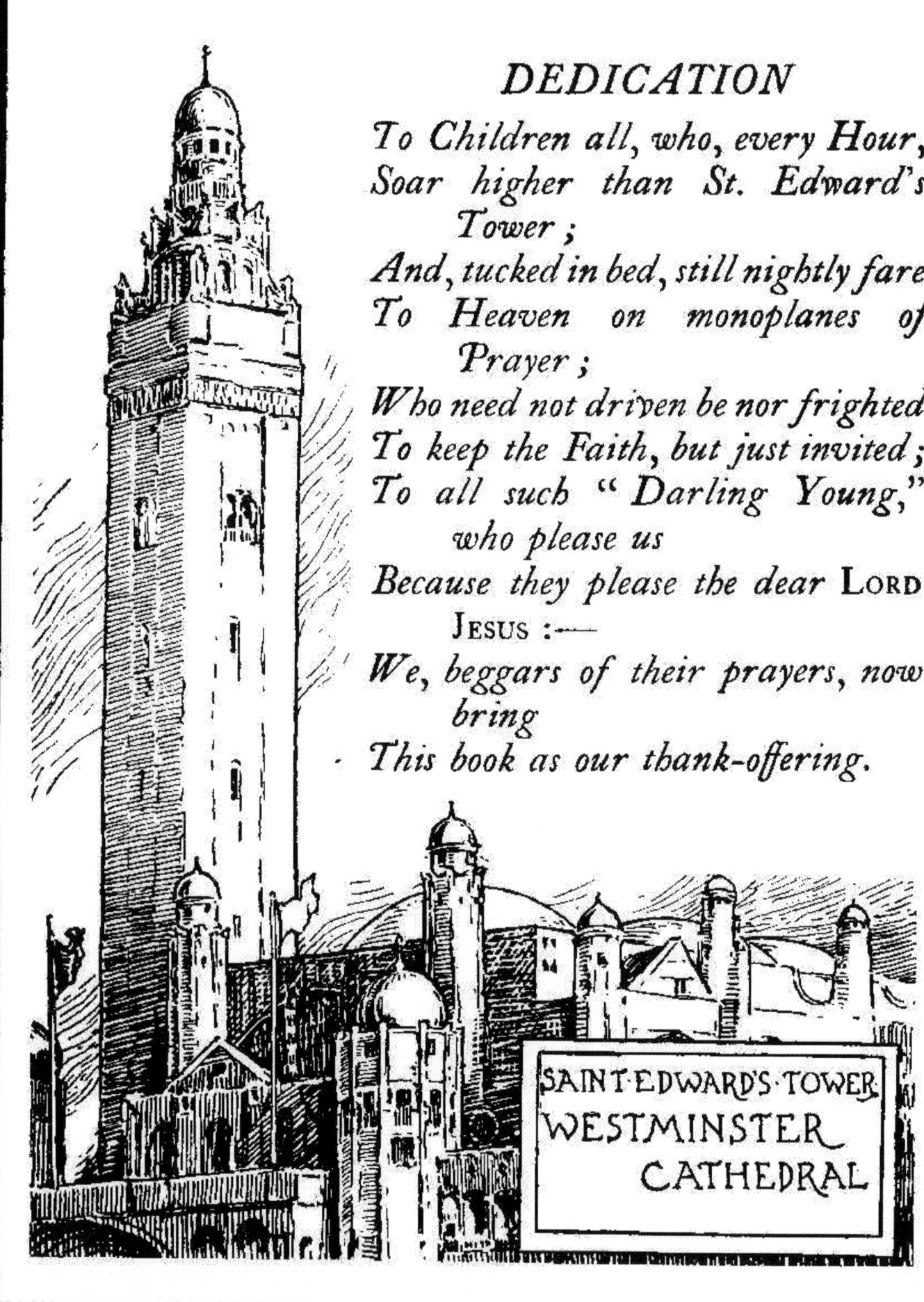

DEDICATION

*To Children all, who, every Hour,
Soar higher than St. Edward's Tower;
And, tucked in bed, still nightly fare
To Heaven on monoplanes of Prayer;
Who need not driven be nor frighted
To keep the Faith, but just invited;
To all such "Darling Young," who please us
Because they please the dear* LORD JESUS:—
*We, beggars of their prayers, now bring
This book as our thank-offering.*

SAINT·EDWARD'S·TOWER
WESTMINSTER
CATHEDRAL

LITTLE JESUS

LITTLE Jesus, wast Thou shy
Once, and just so small as I?
And what did it feel like to be
Out of Heaven, and just like me?
Didst Thou sometimes think of *there*,
And ask where all the angels were?
I should think that I would cry
For my house all made of sky;
I would look about the air,
And wonder where my angels were;
And at waking 'twould distress me—
Not an angel there to dress me!
Hadst Thou ever any toys,
Like us little girls and boys?
And didst Thou play in Heaven with all
The angels that were not too tall,
With stars for marbles? Did the things
Play *Can you see me?* through their wings?

Didst Thou kneel at night to pray,
And didst Thou join Thy hands, this way?
And did they tire sometimes, being young,
And make the prayer seem very long?

And dost Thou like it best, that we
Should join our hands to pray to Thee?
I used to think, before I knew,
The prayer not said unless we do.
And did Thy Mother at the night
Kiss Thee, and fold the clothes in right?
And didst Thou feel quite good in bed,
Kissed, and sweet, and thy prayers said?

Thou canst not have forgotten all
That it feels like to be small:
And Thou know'st I cannot pray
To Thee in my father's way—
When Thou wast so little, say,
Couldst Thou talk Thy Father's way?—

So, a little Child, come down
And hear a child's tongue like Thy own;
Take me by the hand and walk,
And listen to my baby-talk.
To Thy Father show my prayer
(He will look, Thou art so fair),
And say: "O Father, I, Thy Son,
Bring the prayer of a little one."

And He will smile, that children's tongue
Has not changed since Thou wast young!

THE LITTLE SCHOLAR

THERE went a little scholar,
    With slow and lagging feet,
    Towards the great church portal
    That opened in the street.

Without, the sun was shining;
    Within, the air was dim;
He caught a waft of incense,
    A dying note of hymn.

He drew the crimson curtain,
    And cast a look inside,
To where the sunbeam lightened
    The form of Him Who died,
Between St. John and Mary,
    On roodloft crucified.

The curtain fell behind him,
    He stood a little while,
Then signed him with the water,
    And rambled down the aisle.

Behind a great brown pillar
    The scholar took his stand,
And trifled with the ribbon
    Of the satchel in his hand.

His little breast was beating,
    His blue eyes brimming o'er;
Like April rains, his tears
    Fell spangling on the floor.

An aged priest was passing;
    He saw the boy and said,
"Why, little one, this weeping,
    This heavy, hanging head?"

"My Father, O my Father,
    I've sinned," said the child,
"And have no rest of conscience
    Till I am reconciled."

But then a burst of weeping
    And sobs his utterance broke—
The priest could not distinguish
    A single word he spoke.

Then said the pastor gently:
    "You have a little slate—
Write on it the confession
    You are pow'rless to relate."

The child his satchel opened,
   And strove his sin to note,
But still the tear-drops dribbled
   As busily he wrote.

Now when the tale was finished,
   He held it to the priest
With sigh, as from a burden
   He felt himself released.

The old man raised the tablet
   To read what there was set;
But could not, for the writing
   Was blotted with the wet.

Then turned the aged confessor
   Towards the kneeling boy,
With countenance all shining
   In rapture of pure joy.

"Depart in peace, forgiven,
   Away with doubting fears!
Thy sins have all been cancelled
   By the torrent of thy tears."

AT PREGHIERA

A BABY to a Baby prays:
"O Infant Jesus, meek and mild,
From 'mid the glory and the rays,
Look on a little child!"

As one child to another may,
  He talks without a thought of fear;
Commending to a Child to-day
  All that a child holds dear :

His father, mother, brother, nurse,
  His cat, his dog, his bird, his toys—
Things that make up the universe
  Of darling girls and boys.

A child lifts up his little hands
  Unto a Child; and it may be
The Host of Heaven all gazing stands
  That tender sight to see.

CREATION'S CATECHISM

O HAPPY children who can read
  In Nature's book the Christian Creed—
    Their Catechism half rehearse
    In classrooms of the Universe!

  Clean winds that blow on every coast
  Tell secrets of the Holy Ghost;
  In waters everywhere is heard
  Regeneration's whispered word;

The sun, going down in clouds of blood,
Proclaims the Christ upon the Rood;
The sun, uprising from his prison,
Declares the Christ again uprisen—
Then, like a Host is held on high
In the cathedral of the sky,
And glorious Benediction gives
To all that loves, and, loving, lives.

The moon, Our Lady, shining fair,
Her borrowed glory doth declare;
Day's requiem lights, when day doth die,
In fervent stars we may descry—
And, even in a candle's flare,
"A little tongue of burning prayer."

On all the common country sod
We tread the earth Our Saviour trod;
By banks of Liffey, Thames, or Tyne,
Are palmers true in Palestine.
In every tree in every wood
We see the symbol of the Rood—
In every bough's and branch's toss
A brother's beckoning to the Cross;
And hear, in each shy bird that sings,
A Bird of God with shielding wings.

For Heaven plays hourly hide-and-seek
With all earth's company of meek,
Who see Lord Christs in babes the least,
Fore-taste in fields of corn their Feast.

Nick-names like Pantheist, you see,
Need never frighten you and me—
On men and seas and lands who look
As pages of God's Picture-book.

ST. TERESA AND THE CHILD

"WHO art thou, son?" *The little stranger smiled—*
"*And who art THOU?*" Whereto she made reply,
"Teresa I of Jesus am, my child"
He—radiant—"*Jesus of Teresa I.*"

OUT OF BOUNDS

A LITTLE Boy of heavenly birth,
  But far from home to-day,
Comes down to find His ball, the earth,
  That sin has cast away.
O comrades, let us one and all
Join in to get Him back His ball!

Unless you become as little children you shall not enter the Kingdom of Heaven.—*St. Matthew.*

A TALK, WITH TALES & TEXTS, BY FATHER VINCENT McNABB, O.P.

LITTLE JESUS

THE Little Jesus to whom the child in the poem is talking is Little Jesus at Nazareth, not yet old enough to go to school. Let us bow our head at the name JESUS, for this little boy is the GREAT SON OF GOD. Like every great king, He has more than one home. On the side of the hill at Nazareth He has an earthly Home, and in Heaven there is another Home "all made of sky." Mary, our Mother, was His Mother at Nazareth; and God, our Father, was His Father in Heaven. Some day before I die I hope to see Nazareth; but I hope still more to see Heaven after I die.

A priest who is now dead told me he was one day giving catechism to the little soldier boys in the Duke of York's School, Chelsea. They had come to the *Our Father*. Turning to the boys, he said, "Is God the Father everywhere?"

"Yes!" rang out all the little soldiers' voices.

"But if God the Father is everywhere, why don't you say, 'Our Father who art everywhere,' and not 'Our Father who art in heaven?'" asked the priest.

There was silence. Nearly all the little soldier boys looked now at each other and now at the priest, but no one spoke. At last, one boy timidly held up his hand, saying, "Please, Father, I fink I know."

"Well, then, Bobby," said the priest, "tell me. If

Where there are two or three gathered in My Name, there am I in the midst of them.—*St. Matthew.*

God is everywhere and not in heaven only, why do you say, 'Our Father, *who art in heaven?*'"

"''Cos it's 'eadquarters, Father!"

Now, I don't think that St. Thomas Aquinas himself could have answered better than that.

The child in the poem thinks he would be unhappy if Heaven were *his* headquarters and he were away from it.

> And at waking 'twould distress me—
> Not an angel there to dress me.

Do you remember that in one of the Gospels we are told of an angel that came to Little Jesus when He was grown up? It was the last night He was on earth. He went out into the dark olive garden, and spent a long, long time at His night prayers—the last night prayers He ever said. He thought of you and me, and everybody else, and of all our sins. He was so sad that the blood oozed from His brow. Then an angel came to comfort Him. I remember once reading that the dear, loving angel wiped away the blood from His forehead. When you and I are ill, how nice it is to feel the touch of a soft, gentle hand. So now let us both say, "Thank you, dear, gentle Angel. And when I am saying my last night prayers before I die, set thy caressing hand on my brow!"

Which lines of this poem do you really like the best? I think these in which the earthly child asks the Child Jesus:

> And did'st Thou feel quite good in bed,
> Kissed, and sweet, and Thy prayers said?

We are told only twice in the Gospels that any-

> The things that thou hast not gathered in thy youth, how shalt thou find them in thy old age?—*Ecclesiastes.*

one kissed Jesus. We are not told, because we do not want telling, that His Mother and His Guardian, St. Joseph, ever kissed Him. We should want telling if they had not kissed Him. But we are told that St. Mary Magdalen kissed His feet; and Judas Iscariot kissed His cheek. Whenever I think of St. Mary Magdalen, I say, " Thank you, dear St. Mary Magdalen. I am glad someone thought of kissing His feet." Judas was a bad priest, and gave Our Lord a traitor's kiss. That is, perhaps, the reason why, during Holy Mass, the priest to-day, as if to make amends, often kisses the vestments, the altar, the Book, the corporal. Count up how many kisses the priest gives at every Mass.

THE LITTLE SCHOLAR

Everyone will understand and love this poem, in spite of one or two long words, such as "roodloft." In olden days the Churches, instead of having altar rails, had a beautiful screen of stone or wood. On the top was a large crucifix or rood; this creen was called the rood-loft.

If any of you live in London, you can go to the great Cathedral of Westminster. Over the altar rails, and high up in the dim air, is hung a large painted rood or cross, and on it a white figure of Jesus. A few months ago, a father and his little son came in. They were not poor but rich; I mean, they had a great deal of gold, but, as you will see, they were really very, very poor. As soon as the little boy lifted his eyes up, he was startled, for he caught sight of the painted crucifix and the white, stretched figure of Jesus.

"Father, what is that?" he said. "I have never seen

The Lord is the Keeper of Little Ones.—*Psalms.*

anything like that before." He did not know what a crucifix was! Now, you see, why I said they were not really rich, for *his* little son did not know that he was "redeemed, not with corruptible things as gold or silver . . . but with the Precious Blood of Christ." Then the father explained to *his* little son, as your teacher might explain geography to you, what we believe about the Son of God made man;—and walked on. But *his* little son, like the little penitent boy in the poem, could not keep his eyes from the figure on the rood. Again and again the little white face turned towards Jesus on His Cross.

* * * * *

*Thy sins have all been cancelled
By the torrent of thy tears.*

Of course, the old chronicler who first told this story knew very well such a dear little fellow would have no mortal sins, or he must have waited till he could tell them. His deep sorrow and love of Jesus Crucified would wash his venial sins away.

Whosoever shall not receive the Kingdom of God as a little child shall not enter into it.—*St. Mark.*

AT PRAYER

THIS text, and the text printed at the head of the next page, are the Children's Charter, securing them their inheritance in the Kingdom of Heaven: and many a tale teaches the young to remain childlike in their love, in their humility, and in their faith. Here is one such tale.

A soul that had spent fifty years in the burning desert, fasting and praying, knocked after death at the gate of Heaven.

St. Peter, the gate-keeper, said, "What do you seek?"
The soul answered, "To enter within the gates."

Suffer little children to come unto Me, and forbid them not, for of such is the Kingdom of God.—*St. Mark.*

Peter said, "How old are you?"
The soul answered, "Eighty years."
But the gates remained shut.
After a thousand years in Purgatory, the soul knocked once more at the gate of Heaven.
St. Peter said, "What do ye seek?"
The soul answered, "To enter within the gates."
St. Peter said, "How old are you?"
The soul replied, timidly, "I am a little child!"
The gates were opened.

ST. TERESA AND THE CHILD

St. Teresa, because she was a saint, saw Christ in the Child who appeared to her. One point of the parable is that saints see the Christ in every child. They remember how He told His disciples that if they did a service to the least of His little ones they did it to Him.

CREATION'S CATECHISM

We often learn catechism indoors. But these verses tell us how we may learn it outdoors. It is an Open-Air Class. The world with all its hills and seas and flowers and waves and light and dark and sun and moon and stars is a class-room where we may learn the Catechism.

The *Wind* in its comings and goings is likened in Scripture to the Holy Ghost, Who "breatheth where He will, and thou hearest His voice, but thou knowest not whence He cometh and whither He goeth." He sometimes comes as a gentle breeze stirring the tree-tops, scattering the pollen that

Fear not, little Flock, for it hath pleased your Father to give you a Kingdom.—*St. Luke.*

fertilizes ; sometimes as a great whirlwind, driving before it the leaves as though they were the wicked fleeing before His wrath. The *Water* is a faithful servant for cleansing, and tells us how Jesus cleansed our sins and redeemed us. It tells us, too, of our Baptism. *Sunset* is like the daily death of the Sun. When we see it we think of the death of Jesus. *Sunrise* is like the daily resurrection of the Sun. When we see it we remember Easter morning. The *Moon* borrows her light from the Sun as Mary, the Mother of Jesus, borrows all her grace and all her holiness from her Child, Jesus.

*** A Pantheist is one who thinks God is everything. But we think only that God is *everywhere*. Creation groaned for His coming, says St. Paul ; and, in joy of Him, the little hills clapped their hands, and the morning stars, each in his station, sang together.

THE Earth is round ; so this poet, who was a priest too, calls it a ball—the ball which the Boy Christ has lost because it is in sin, but which He wants to get back, and wants us to help Him to get back.

OUT OF BOUNDS

Our Blessed Lord, speaking to tradesmen, called life a trade, in which, He said, a man might make a hundred-fold, that is, 10,000 per cent !—ten hundred thousand pounds for every hundred pounds he traded with.

One of the English Martyrs (the Ven. John Pibush, S.J.) called life a game of Football. He said that any priest who came to England must give up all games but football, which is made up of pushes and kicks.

27

It is not the will of your Father who is in Heaven that one of these little ones should perish.—*St. Matthew.*

Your life and mine, dear reader, is a game. It is just like every other outdoor game, because there are hard knocks and risks to put up with. One thing is peculiar to it. We never know when it will end. But you will pray for me, and I for you, so that when the Angel of Death rings and the game is over, we may be taken to Jesus, the Little Child Who is our Onlooker and Referee and Captain and Judge and King and Prize, for ever and ever. Amen.

THANKS

The verses which we have called, from their opening words, LITTLE JESUS, were first called by their writer, Francis Thompson, EX ORE INFANTIUM, He meant us to remember our Blessed Lord's words, "Out of the mouth of babes . . Thou hast perfected praise." ⁋⁋ The writer of CREATION'S CATECHISM has tried to see Nature as Francis Thompson saw it ; to look on God's handiwork through the eyes of a poet, and to translate his visions into common speech. Francis Thompson died in 1907. May he rest in peace. ⁋⁋⁋ To Messrs. Macmillan, the publishers of the old story, THE LITTLE SCHOLAR, borrowed from mediæval Germany, and to Mr. Baring-Gould—thanks ! ⁋⁋⁋ To Mrs. Katharine Tynan Hinkson, beloved of readers young and old — thanks !

The Children's Hour of Heaven on Earth

First Published 1913 by P.J. Kenedy

Reprinted 2007 by Catholic Authors Press

International Standard Book Number: 978-0-9782985-2-4

Catholic Authors Press 2007

books@catholicauthors.org

www.CatholicAuthors.org

THE CHILDREN'S HOUR
of Heaven *on* Earth

P. J. Kenedy & Sons
44 Barclay Street, New York

CATHOLIC AUTHORS PRESS

Catholic Authors Press is dedicated to promoting preserving our rich Roman Catholic literary heritage. Catholic Authors does this through the rescue and recirculation of used and out-of-print books as well as the publishing of rare and classic titles from the past for the next generation of faithful. Catholic Authors maintains a comprehensive biographical database of Catholic writers accessible online for free and plans to offer workshops for young and aspiring Catholic writers in answer to the plea of Pope Pius XI: "In vain do you build schools and churches if at the same time you do not also build up a good Catholic literature."